Kobus Genis

MEET
GOD

Through the NARRATIVES and LAW

MODULE 2

In memory of my parents, Koos and Malie Genis, who instilled the love for the Bible in me.

CONTENTS

INTRODUCTION

Video material of all lessons is available at
https://biblegps.teachable.com
COUPON to waive Video fees: <u>See last page!</u>

Welcome to Module Two. I am so excited that you have decided to continue with the "Meet God" series.

In this Module we will apply the Bible GPS method of understanding, application and communication to two different types of literature namely the Narratives and the Law.

That means we will cover a substantial portion of the Old Testament. You will discover how the Old Testament is still applicable to us in the 21st century.

Why should we study the Old Testament now that we have the New Testament?

The Old Testament lays the foundation for the teachings and events found in the New Testament. The Bible is a progressive revelation. If you skip the first half of any good book and try to finish it, you will have a hard time understanding the characters, the plot, and the ending. In the same way, the New Testament is only completely understood when it is read with the Old Testament as a backdrop.

I like what Bono had to say about the Old Testament: "I accept the Old Testament as more of an action movie: blood, car chases, evacuations, a lot of special effects, seas dividing, mass murder, adultery. The children of God are running amok, wayward. Maybe that's why they're so relatable."

Lesson 1 deals with how to interpret the Narratives of the Bible.

In **Lesson 2** we will apply the GPS-method to Genesis 39:1-23.

In **Lesson 3** we will apply the GPS-method to Ruth 2:1-13.

Lesson 4 deals with how to interpret the Law of the Bible.

In **Lessons 5** we will apply the GPS-method to Leviticus 19:9-14.

In **Lessons 6** we will apply the GPS-Method to Deuteronomy 15:12-17

Objective of Module 2

- To understand how to interpret Narratives and the Law parts of the Bible.

- To apply the Bible GPS-method to passages from the Narratives as well as the Law.

LESSON 1
THE NARRATIVES

Purpose
To get a better understanding of the Narratives

Introductory Remarks

Over _____ of the biblical material is narrative, story, and it is the most common single type of writing in the Bible.

The Nature of Narratives

The **purpose** of narratives

- _____

- _____

- _____

All narratives have _____ and a _____.

Characters

God is always the _____ character of Scripture; it is God's story.

The Plot

The plot is the way in which a narrative develops and serves to capture the _____ of the audience.

There is always an element which _____ tension as well as an element which _____ tension.

Element which creates tension	Element which releases tension
Plan	Execution
Mystery	Explanation
Problem	Resolution

The **problem–resolution** structure is the _____ in the Bible's narratives.

The execution, explanation and resolution are normally followed with a _____.

An Example of a problem–resolution structure:

Joshua 2:1-15 (Rahab and the spies)

Tension (Problem) Two spies and a prostitute in one room (verses 1-3)

[1] Then Joshua son of Nun secretly sent two spies from Shittim. "Go, look over the land," he said, "especially Jericho." So they went and entered the house of a prostitute named Rahab and stayed there.[2] The king of Jericho was told, "Look, some of the Israelites have come here tonight to spy out the land." [3] So the king of Jericho sent this message to Rahab:
"Bring out the men who came to you and entered your house, because they have come to spy out the whole land."

Release of tension (Resolution) The prostitute acts wisely (verses 4-6)

[4] But the woman had taken the two men and hidden them. She said, "Yes, the men came to me, but I did not know where they had come from.

Result: An agreement involving mutual trust (verses 7-15)

[7] So the men set out in pursuit of the spies on the road that leads to the fords of the Jordan, and as soon as the pursuers had gone out, the gate was shut. [8] Before the spies lay down for the night, she went up on the roof [9]and said to them, "I know that the Lord has given you this land and that a great fear of you has fallen on us, so that all who live in this country are melting in fear because of you. [12] "Now then, please swear to me by the Lord that you will show kindness to my family, because I have shown kindness to you. [15] So she let them down by a rope through the window, for the house she lived in was part of the city wall. (NIV)

Three Levels of Narratives

1. The _____ *level* is that of the whole universal plan of God, the big story of Scripture.

2. The _____ *level* centers on Israel.

3. The _____ *level* comprises of all the hundreds of individual narratives that make up the other two levels.

The individual narratives can be divided into _____. An episode is a chain of events that are related, having the same location, time, and major participants.

For example, in the Joseph narrative (Genesis 37-50) we have many individual narratives which are divided into episodes like:

Episode 1: Joseph's dreams (37:1-11)

Episode 2: Joseph sold by his brothers (37:12-36)

Episode 3: Joseph and Pothiphar's wife (39:1-23)

Episode 4: The cupbearer and the baker (40:1-23)

Every individual Old Testament narrative (bottom level) is at least a part of the greater narrative of Israel's history in the world (the middle level), which in turn is a part of the ultimate narrative of God's creation and his redemption of it (the top level).[1]

---

1. Gordon D. Fee & Douglas Stuart, *How to Read the Bible For All Its Worth,* 2nd edn. (Grand Rapids: Zondervan, 1993), 91-92

A Few Principles for Interpreting Narratives

1. Narratives record what happened – not necessarily what should have happened or what ought to happen every time. Therefore, not every narrative has an identifiable _____ of the story.

2. What people do in narratives is not necessarily a _____ example for us.

3. We are not always told whether what happened was _____ or _____.
We are expected to be able to judge that on the basis of what God has taught elsewhere in scripture.

4. Narratives do not always teach directly. The message of a Narrative is _____.

5. In the final analysis, God is the _____ of all Biblical narratives.[1]

---

1. Gordon D. Fee & Douglas Stuart, *How to Read the Bible For All Its Worth,* 2nd edn. (Grand Rapids: Zondervan, 1993), 91-92

Read the following story about the bear and the two friends:

Two friends were once walking through the forest. They knew that at any time in the forest something dangerous could happen to them. So they promised each other that they would remain united in the face of danger.

Suddenly, they saw a large bear approaching them. One of the friends at once climbed a nearby tree. But the other one did not know how to climb. So being led by his common sense, he lay down on the ground breathless, pretending to be a dead man. He knew that a bear does not eat a dead body. The bear came over and sniffed his face and went away thinking, "he is dead."

The other friend came down from the tree and asked, "Was the bear talking to you?" "Yeah, the bear bent down and whispered in
my ears," said the first friend.
The other friend asked "What did the bear say?" The first friend replied, "The person in the tree is not a good friend."

1. What do you think is the message of this story?

_____

2. Which parts of the story make it interesting and help us to understand the message?

_____

.

3. Would you have arrived at the message by only reading the first two paragraphs?

_____

4. What are the implications of your answer above for your understanding of Biblical narratives?

_____

How to analyze the Narratives?

1. Divide the narrative into _____

Reason: It is easier to understand the message if you divide the narrative into episodes because episodes are usually related.

- **An episode is a chain of events that are related, having the same location, time, and major participants.**

Joshua 2:1-15 is an episode within the narrative.

Outline of Joshua
- The Entrance into the Land (1:1—5:12)
- The Conquest of the Land (5:13—12:24)
- The Distribution of the Land (chs. 13–21)
- Epilogue: Tribal Unity and Loyalty to the Lord (chs. 22–24)

3.2 Determine the _____

Reason: The plot is the way in which the narrative develops.

Determine the plot-structure of Joshua 2:1-15. Indicate the verses that represent the plot-structure.

a) Tension _____
b) Release of tension _____
c) Result _____

3.3 Identify the main _____

Reason: The plot revolves around its characters and their relationships.

Identify the main characters in this episode.

_____

3.4 How does this narrative (_____ level) relate to the narrative of Israel (middle _____) as well as the narrative of God's universal plan of redemption (_____ level)?

Mutual trust between Rahab and the two spies (**bottom level**) has helped the Israelites to enter the Promised Land (**middle level**), It is wondrous that Rahab also experienced God's goodness when she was included in the genealogy of Jesus - Matt. 1:5 (**top level**).

3.5 Conclude and summarize the message to the _____ _____.

"Goodness is the only investment which never fails."
Henry David Thoreau

Joshua 2:1-15 (Prose: Narrative) Rahab and the spies

[1]Then Joshua son of Nun secretly sent two spies from Shittim. "Go, look over the land," he said, "especially Jericho." So they went and entered the house of a prostitute named Rahab and stayed there.

[2] The king of Jericho was told, "Look, some of the Israelites have come here tonight to spy out the land." [3] So the king of Jericho sent this message to Rahab: "Bring out the men who came to you and entered your house, because they have come to spy out the whole land."

[4] But the woman had taken the two men and hidden them. She said, "Yes, the men came to me, but I did not know where they had come from. [5] At dusk, when it was time to close the city gate, they left. I don't know which way they went. Go after them quickly. You may catch up with them." [6] (But she had taken them up to the roof and hidden them under the stalks of flax she had laid out on the roof.) [7] So the men set out in pursuit of the spies on the road that leads to the fords of the Jordan, and as soon as the pursuers had gone out, the gate was shut.

[8] Before the spies lay down for the night, she went up on the roof [9] and said to them, "I know that the Lord has given you this land and that a great fear of you has fallen on us, so that all who live in this country are melting in fear because of you. [10] We have heard how the Lord dried up the water of the Red Sea for you when you came out of Egypt, and what you did to Sihon and Og, the two kings of the Amorites east of the Jordan, whom you completely destroyed.[b] [11] When we heard of it, our hearts melted in fear and everyone's courage failed because of you, for the Lord your God is God in heaven above and on the earth below.

[12] "Now then, please swear to me by the Lord that you will show kindness to my family, because I have shown kindness to you. Give me a sure sign [13] that you will spare the lives of my father and mother, my brothers and sisters, and all who belong to them—and that you will save us from death."

[14] "Our lives for your lives!" the men assured her. "If you don't tell what we are doing, we will treat you kindly and faithfully when the Lord gives us the land."

[15] So she let them down by a rope through the window, for the house she lived in was part of the city wall. (NIV)

Questions for Group Discussion

- Did the lesson help you to get a better understanding of the Narratives?

- What touched you the most in the lesson?

- Is there anything in the lesson that was not clear to you? If so, what was unclear?

- Share blessings and prayer requests and pray for one another.

LESSON 2
THE GPS-METHOD APPLIED TO Genesis 39:1-23

Purpose
To apply the GPS-Method to Genesis 39:1-23

The Bible GPS-Method takes us through the processes of UNDERSTANDING, APPLICATION AND COMMUNICATION

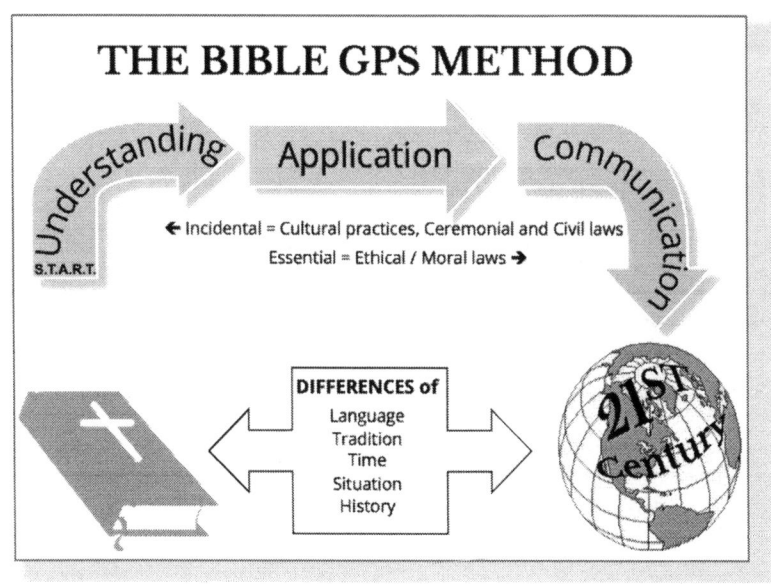

Genesis 39:1-23

[1] "Now Joseph had been taken down to Egypt. Potiphar, an Egyptian who was one of Pharaoh's officials, the captain of the guard, bought him from the Ishmaelites who had taken him there.

[2] The Lord was with Joseph so that he prospered, and he lived in the house of his Egyptian master. [3] When his master saw that the Lord was with him and that the Lord gave him success in everything he did, [4] Joseph found favor in his eyes and became his attendant. Potiphar put him in charge of his household, and he entrusted to his care everything he owned.
[5] From the time he put him in charge of his household and of all that he owned, the Lord blessed the household of the Egyptian because of Joseph. The blessing of the Lord was on everything Potiphar had, both in the house and in the field. [6] So Potiphar left everything he had in Joseph's care; with Joseph in charge, he did not concern himself with anything except the food he ate.

Now Joseph was well-built and handsome, [7] and after a while his master's wife took notice of Joseph and said, "Come to bed with me!"

[8] But he refused. "With me in charge," he told her, "my master does not concern himself with anything in the house; everything he owns he has entrusted to my care. [9] No one is greater in this house than I am. My master has withheld nothing from me except you, because you are his wife. How then could I do such a wicked thing and sin against God?" [10] And though she spoke to Joseph day after day, he refused to go to bed with her or even be with her.

[11] One day he went into the house to attend to his duties, and none of the household servants was inside. [12] She caught him by his cloak and said, "Come to bed with me!" But he left his cloak in her hand and ran out of the house.

[13] When she saw that he had left his cloak in her hand and had run out of the house, [14] she called her household servants. "Look," she said to them, "this Hebrew has been brought to us to make sport of us! He came in here to sleep with me, but I screamed. [15] When he heard me scream for help, he left his cloak beside me and ran out of the house."

[16] She kept his cloak beside her until his master came home. [17] Then she told him this story: "That Hebrew slave you brought us came to me to make sport of me. [18] But as soon as I screamed for help, he left his cloak beside me and ran out of the house."

[19] When his master heard the story his wife told him, saying, "This is how your slave treated me," he burned with anger. [20] Joseph's master took him and put him in prison, the place where the king's prisoners were confined.

But while Joseph was there in the prison, [21] the Lord was with him; he showed him kindness and granted him favor in the eyes of the prison warden. [22] So the warden put Joseph in charge of all those held in the prison, and he was made responsible for all that was done there. [23] The warden paid no attention to anything under Joseph's care, because the Lord was with Joseph and gave him success in whatever he did." (NIV)

A. THE PROCESS OF UNDERSTANDING (S.T.A.R.T.)

1. SITUATION

The context of a passage will help you better understand the text. You can get the information from a Study Bible, Bible commentaries or from the Internet: http://www.biblestudytools.com/genesis/

- **What was the purpose of the book?**

  _____

- **Who was the Sender and Receiver?**

  _____

- **Where does the passage fit in the structure (division) of the specific book?**

  A. Creation (1:1—2:3)
  B. Pre-history (2:4—11:26)
  C. Patriarchal History (11:27—50:26)

- Where does the passage fit in the structure (division) of the Bible?

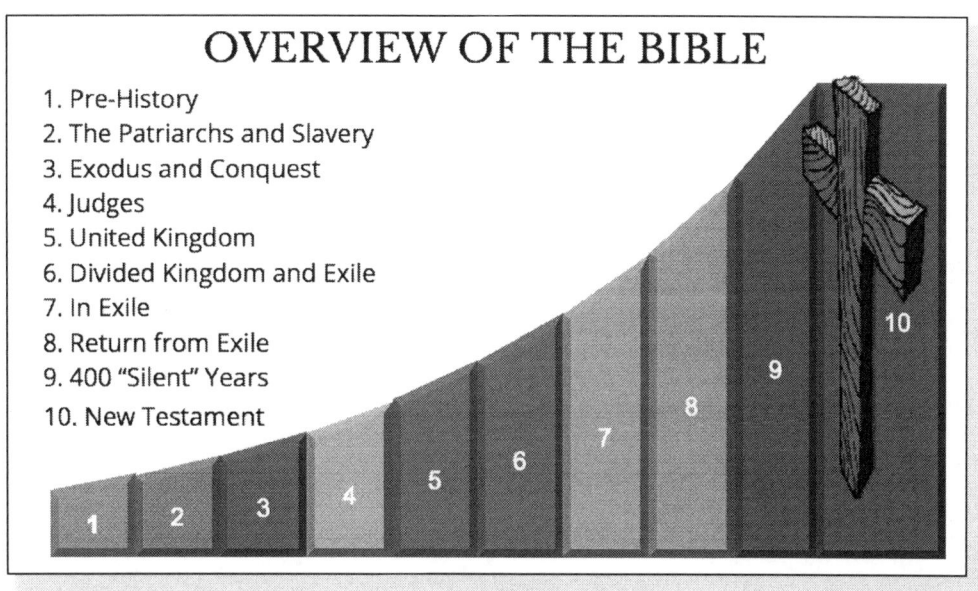

OVERVIEW OF THE BIBLE

1. Pre-History
2. The Patriarchs and Slavery
3. Exodus and Conquest
4. Judges
5. United Kingdom
6. Divided Kingdom and Exile
7. In Exile
8. Return from Exile
9. 400 "Silent" Years
10. New Testament

- When did the book originate?

_____

- Placing of the book?

_____

- Important characters

_____

- Distinctive features

_____

2. TYPE OF LITERATURE

The type of literature will determine how you will analyze the passage.

PROSE	POETRY
Narrative/History The Law Prophecy Gospel Epistle (Letter) Apocalyptic Writing	Wisdom Psalms Prophecy

What type of literature is Genesis 39:1-23?

_____

3. ANALYSIS OF THE PASSAGE

3.1 Divide the narrative into episodes

Reason: It is easier to understand the message if you divide the narrative into episodes because episodes are usually related.

An episode is a chain of events that are related, having the same location, time, and major participants.

Genesis 39:1-23 is an episode within the narrative.

Outline of Genesis
1. Creation (1:1—2:3)
2. Pre-History (2:4—11:26)
    i.   Adam and Eve in Eden (2:4–25)
    ii.   The Fall and Its Consequences (ch. 3)
    iii.   Sin's Progression (4:1–16)
    iv.   The Genealogy of Cain (4:17–26)
    v.   The Genealogy of Seth (ch. 5)
    vi.   God's Response to Human Depravity (6:1–8)
    vii.   The Great Flood (6:9—9:29)
    viii.   The Spread of the Nations (10:1—11:26)

3. Patriarchal History (11:27—50:26)
    i.   The Life of Abraham (11:27—25:11)
    ii.   The Descendants of Ishmael (25:12–18).
    iii.   The Life of Jacob (25:19—35:29)
    iv.   The Descendants of Esau (36:1—37:1)
    v.   The Life of Joseph (37:2—50:26)

3.2 Determine the plot-structure

Reason: The plot is the way in which the narrative develops.

The plot-structre usually is:

1. Tension
2. Release of tension
3. Result

Determine the plot-structure of Genesis 39:1-23. Indicate the verses that represent the plot-structure.

1. Tension _____
2. Release of tension _____
3. Result _____

3.3 Identify the main characters

Reason: The plot revolves around its characters and their relationships.

Identify the main characters in this episode.

_____

3.4 How does this narrative (bottom level) relate to the narrative of Israel (middle level) as well as the narrative of God's universal plan of redemption (top level)?

Joseph's obedience (**bottom level**) has prepared him to rise to the top in Egypt and later to help save Israel from famine and to bring the entire family of Jacob (Israel) to Egypt (**middle level**), thus fulfilling God's will - see Genesis 15:12-16 (**top level**).

3.5 Conclude and summarize the message to the original receiver.

This is not always easy because in the narratives the message is often **implied**. Narratives do not always teach directly.

This narrative shows us the importance of trust. Without trust we cannot build healthy relationships. This narrative does not ask us to consider whether we can trust people, but rather if we can be trusted. God always works graciously behind the scenes.

4. RELATIONSHIP TO THE REST OF THE BIBLE

Does the message in Genesis 39:1-23 relate to the rest of the Bible?

Read the following passages to determine your answer:

Proverbs 3:5-6 (NIV)
"[5]Trust in the Lord with all your heart
and lean not on your own understanding;
[6] in all your ways submit to him,
and he will make your paths straight."

Romans 8:28 (NIV)
"And we know that in all things God works for the good of those who love him, who have been called according to his purpose."

YES _____ NO _____

5. TEST OF YOUR FINDINGS

Do the findings of other sources (e.g., commentaries, Study Bibles) confirm the message to the original receiver?

YES _____ NO _____

B. THE PROCESS OF APPLICATION

In this process, we determine whether or not the message to the original receiver is still applicable (essential or incidental) to our present situation.

You must distinguish the difference between an INCIDENTAL and an ESSENTIAL message.

We saw in Module 1, Lesson 4 that only the Moral (Ethical) Laws are essential and, therefore, applicable to us.

Civil Laws	Ceremonial Laws	Cultural Practices	Moral Laws

PURPOSE

Regulating the nation of Israel	Animal sacrifices to make atonement for sin. Point to Christ, the true Lamb	Comprise the ways people do certain things	Universal guidelines telling us how to live

EXAMPLE

Building regulations (Deut 22:8)	The Passover (Lev 16)	To greet with a kiss. (1 Peter 5:14)	The Ten Commandments (Ex 20)

Is the message to the original receivers applicable to us in the 21st century?

YES _____ NO _____

C. THE PROCESSES OF COMMUNICATION

In this process we communicate the message to a specific target group.

Read this devotional.

Everyone faces temptations. A temptation is the desire to have or do something that you know you should avoid.

Joseph can help us to deal with temptation. Joseph was Potiphar's (he was the captain of Pharaoh's guard) personal attendant.

Potiphar's wife starts flirting with Joseph. She makes attempts to seduce him into sleeping with her.   After all, Joseph is muscular and well built. Joseph resists the temptation by running away from it. Temptations normally start with a harmless thought. Then you start to entertain that thought. Then you commit the act. Joseph didn't entertain the temptation.

I know it is not always easy. Maybe you are in the grip of something you know is harmful. Talk to someone you can trust! No one is perfect! We all make mistakes!

(Taken from the Devotional "@GodsTweet")

Questions for Group Discussion

1. What type of conflicting emotions do you imagine Joseph dealt with while being pursued by Potiphar's insistent wife day after day?

_____

_____

2. Why is it so easy to fall or give in to temptation? Why do we have a constant struggle with sin?

_____

_____

3. Can temptation be considered as sin? (Matt. 4:1-11; Heb. 4:15)

_____

_____

4. Read James 1:13-15

[13] "When tempted, no one should say, "God is tempting me." For God cannot be tempted by evil, nor does he tempt anyone; [14] but each person is tempted when they are dragged away by their own evil desire and enticed. [15] Then, after desire has conceived, it gives birth to sin; and sin, when it is full-grown, gives birth to death." (NIV)

What does this passage teach us about temptation?

_____

_____

5. What can we learn from Genesis 39 about how we can overcome temptation?

_____

_____

6. Share blessings and prayer requests and pray for one another.

"If you don't want temptation to follow you, don't act as if you're interested."
Author Unknown

LESSON 3
THE GPS-METHOD APPLIED TO RUTH 2:1-13

Purpose
To apply the GPS-Method to Ruth 2:1-10

The Bible GPS-Method takes us through the processes of UNDERSTANDING, APPLICATION AND COMMUNICATION

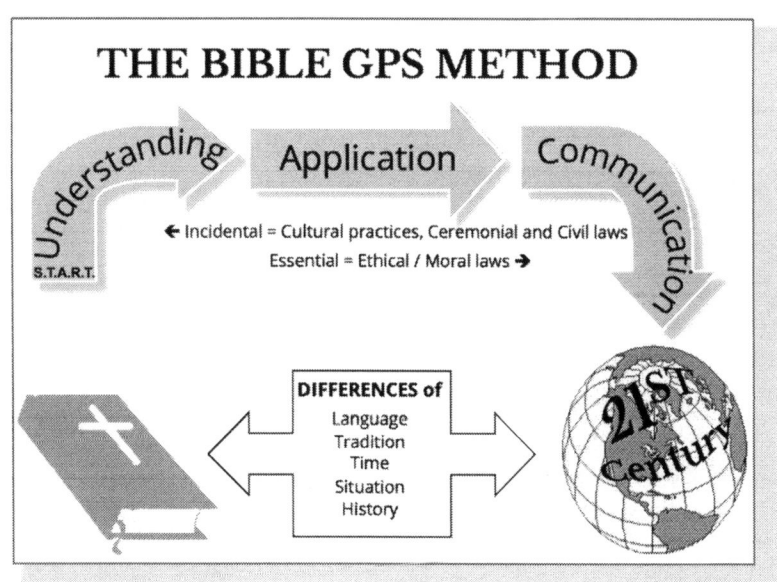

Ruth 2:1-13

[1] "Now there was a wealthy and influential man in Bethlehem named Boaz, who was a relative of Naomi's husband, Elimelech.

[2] One day Ruth the Moabite said to Naomi, "Let me go out into the harvest fields to pick up the stalks of grain left behind by anyone who is kind enough to let me do it." Naomi replied, "All right, my daughter, go ahead." [3] So Ruth went out to gather grain behind the harvesters. And as it happened, she found herself working in a field that belonged to Boaz, the relative of her father-in-law, Elimelech.

[4] While she was there, Boaz arrived from Bethlehem and greeted the harvesters. "The Lord be with you!" he said. "The Lord bless you!" the harvesters replied.

[5] Then Boaz asked his foreman, "Who is that young woman over there? Who does she belong to?"

[6] And the foreman replied, "She is the young woman from Moab who came back with Naomi. [7] She asked me this morning if she could gather grain behind the harvesters. She has been hard at work ever since, except for a few minutes' rest in the shelter."

[8] Boaz went over and said to Ruth, "Listen, my daughter. Stay right here with us when you gather grain; don't go to any other fields. Stay right behind the young women working in my field. [9] See which part of the field they are harvesting, and then follow them. I have warned the young men not to treat you roughly. And when you are thirsty, help yourself to the water they have drawn from the well."

[10] Ruth fell at his feet and thanked him warmly. "What have I done to deserve such kindness?" she asked. "I am only a foreigner."

[11] "Yes, I know," Boaz replied. "But I also know about everything you have done for your mother-in-law since the death of your husband. I have heard how you left your father and mother and your own land to live here among complete strangers. [12] May the Lord, the God of Israel, under whose wings you have come to take refuge, reward you fully for what you have done."

[13] "I hope I continue to please you, sir," she replied. "You have comforted me by speaking so kindly to me, even though I am not one of your workers." (NLT)

A. THE PROCESS OF UNDERSTANDING (S.T.A.R.T.)

1. SITUATION

The context of a passage will help you better understand the text. You can get the information from a Study Bible, Bible commentaries or from the Internet: http://www.biblestudytools.com/ruth/

- What was the purpose of the book?

  _____

- Who was the Sender and Receiver?

  _____

- Where does the passage fit in the structure (division) of the specific book?

  A. Introduction: Naomi Emptied (1:1–5)
  B. Naomi Returns from Moab (1:6–22)
  C. Ruth and Boaz Meet in the Harvest Fields (ch. 2)
  D. Naomi Sends Ruth to Boaz's Threshing Floor (ch. 3)
  E. Boaz Arranges to Fulfill His Pledge (4:1–12)
  F. Conclusion: Naomi Filled (4:13–17)

- Where does the passage fit in the structure (division) of the Bible?

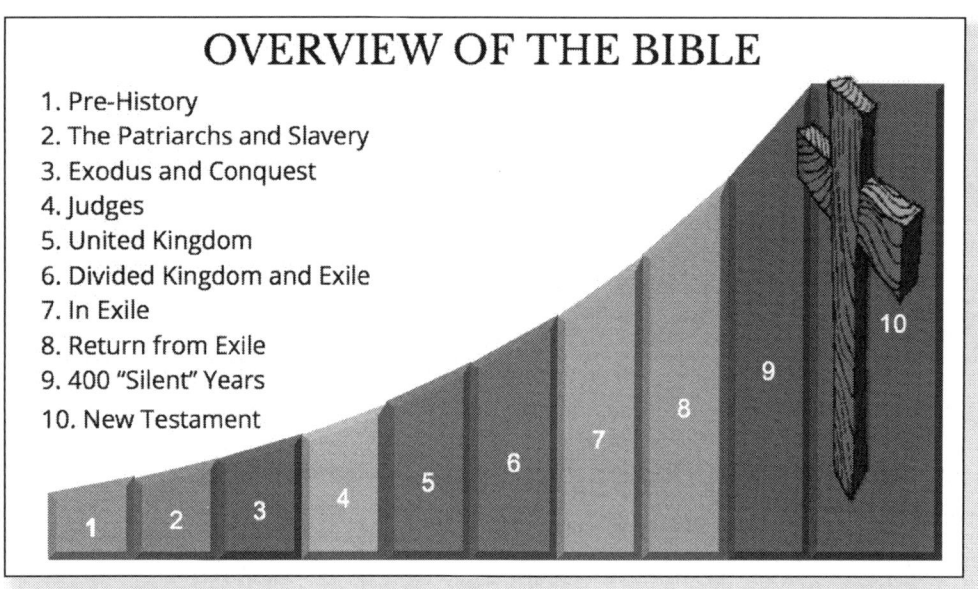

OVERVIEW OF THE BIBLE

1. Pre-History
2. The Patriarchs and Slavery
3. Exodus and Conquest
4. Judges
5. United Kingdom
6. Divided Kingdom and Exile
7. In Exile
8. Return from Exile
9. 400 "Silent" Years
10. New Testament

- When did the book originate?

_____

- Placing of the book?

_____

- Important characters

_____

- Distinctive features

_____

2. TYPE OF LITERATURE

The type of literature will determine how you will analyze the passage.

PROSE	POETRY
Narrative/History The Law Prophecy Gospel Epistle (Letter) Apocalyptic Writing	Wisdom Psalms Prophecy

What type of literature is Ruth 2:1-13?

_____

3. ANALYSIS OF THE PASSAGE

3.1 Divide the narrative into episodes

Reason: It is easier to understand the message if you divide the narrative into episodes because episodes are usually related.

An episode is a chain of events that are related, having the same location, time, and major participants.

Ruth 2:1-13 is an episode within the narrative.

Outline of Ruth
1. Introduction: Naomi Bereft of Family (1:1-5)
2. Episode 1: Naomi Returns to Bethlehem with Ruth (1:6-22)
3. **Episode 2: Ruth Gleans in Boaz's Field** (2:1-23)
4. Episode 3: Ruth, at the Threshing Floor, Asks Boaz to Marry Her (3:1-18)
5. Episode 4: Boaz Arranges Redemption at the Gate (4:1-12)
6. Episode 5: Naomi Blessed with a New Family (4:13-17)
7. Genealogy: Extended Blessing (4:18-22)

3.2 Determine the plot-structure

Reason: The plot is the way in which the narrative develops.

The plot-structre usually is:

- Tension
- Release of tension
- Result

Determine the plot-structure of Ruth 2:1-13. Indicate the verses that represent the plot-structure.

- Tension _____
- Release of tension _____
- Result _____

3.3 Identify the main characters

Reason: The plot revolves around its characters and their relationships.

Identify the main characters in this episode.

_____

3.4 How does this narrative (bottom level) relate to the narrative of Israel (middle level) as well as the narrative of God's universal plan of redemption (top level)?

Ruth's loyalty to Naomi and faith in God (**bottom level**) was in stark contrast to Israel's disloyalty to God (**middle level**). In spite of the initiatives of the people in this narrative it was God who was working behind the scenes and made Ruth and her child, Obed, part of the ancestors of Jesus - Matt. 1:5 (**top level**).

3.5 Conclude and summarize the message to the original receiver.

This is not always easy because in the narratives the message is often **implied**. Narratives do not always teach directly.

This narrative shows us the importance of taking responsibility for our situation and being willing to get out of our comfort zone to do something about it, without noticing God is working behind the scenes to bring about relief.

4. RELATIONSHIP TO THE REST OF THE BIBLE

Does the message in Ruth 2:1-13 relate to the rest of the Bible?

Read the following passages to determine your answer:

Joshua 1:7-9 (NIV)
[7] "Be strong and very courageous. Be careful to obey all the law my servant Moses gave you; do not turn from it to the right or to the left, that you may be successful wherever you go. [8] Keep this Book of the Law always on your lips; meditate on it day and night, so that you may be careful to do everything written in it. Then you will be prosperous and successful. [9] Have I not commanded you? Be strong and courageous. Do not be afraid; do not be discouraged, for the Lord your God will be with you wherever you go."

Proverbs 16:1,9 (NLT)
" [1] We can make our own plans,
but the Lord gives the right answer.
[9] We can make our plans,
but the Lord determines our steps."

Proverbs 27:10 (NLT)

"Never abandon a friend—
either yours or your father's.
When disaster strikes, you won't have to ask your brother for assistance.
It's better to go to a neighbor than to a brother who lives far away."

Romans 8:28 (NLT)

"And we know that God causes everything to work together for the good of those who love God and are called according to his purpose for them."

YES _____ NO _____

5. TEST OF YOUR FINDINGS

Do the findings of other sources (e.g., commentaries, Study Bibles) confirm the message to the original receiver?

YES _____ NO _____

B. THE PROCESS OF APPLICATION

In this process, we determine whether or not the message to the original receiver is still applicable (essential or incidental) to our present situation.

You must distinguish the difference between an INCIDENTAL and an ESSENTIAL message.

We saw in Module 1, Lesson 4 that only the Moral (Ethical) Laws are essential and, therefore, applicable to us.

Civil Laws	Ceremonial Laws	Cultural Practices	Moral Laws

PURPOSE

Regulating the nation of Israel	Animal sacrifices to make atonement for sin. Point to Christ, the true Lamb	Comprise the ways people do certain things	Universal guidelines telling us how to live

EXAMPLE

Building regulations (Deut 22:8)	The Passover (Lev 16)	To greet with a kiss. (1 Peter 5:14)	The Ten Commandments (Ex 20)

Is the message to the original receivers applicable to us in the 21st century?

YES _____ NO _____

C. THE PROCESSES OF COMMUNICATION

In this process we communicate the message to a specific target group.

Read this devotional.

Merciful Coincidences!

Why are God's workings not always evident in our lives? If we want to answer this question, we first have to understand how God works. Without us knowing it, God might be busy in our present situations. This episode in Ruth 2 provides more insight into the way God works in our lives.

The solution to Naomi's problems lies in ordinary events. Nothing sensational happens. Ruth takes the initiative by asking her mother-in-law if she could glean some grain in the fields of someone who will be sympathetic towards her. She takes the initiative and accepts responsibility for her situation. After this, a few events take place—things that one would normally call "coincidences." She "coincidently" goes to the land that belongs to Boaz, who "coincidently" is Naomi's only relative – and also very rich. It is also a "coincidence" that he is unmarried and shows interest in Ruth, a woman from a foreign land. "Coincidently" Boaz arrives on the day she is harvesting the leftover grain. It is a "coincidence" that he notices her and asks questions about her.

In the next episode, we read that Boaz shows mercy towards her. This episode teaches us that we can solve our problems if we follow Ruth's example, namely to take responsibility for our situation and be willing to do something about it. Without us noticing it, God uses people and ordinary events to bring about relief. We often attribute this to "coincidence," but in actual fact it is God who is working behind the scenes.

(Taken from the Devotional "From a Garden to a City.")

Questions for Group Discussion

1. What can we learn from this narrative about God's presence and His working in our lives?

_____

_____

2. How does this narrative relate (bottom level) to the narrative of Israel (middle level) as well as God's big story of redemption (top level)?

_____

_____

3. God is the hero of Biblical narratives. How is God the hero in the Ruth narrative?

_____

_____

4. In what ways is God working gracefully in the shadows of your life?

_____

_____

5. Share blessings and prayer requests and pray for one another.

"Coincidence is God's way of staying anonymous."
Author Unknown

LESSON 4
HOW TO INTERPRET THE LAW

Purpose
To learn the skill of interpreting the Law

Introductory remarks

Following the Exodus out of Egypt God had given the law and a precise set of instructions for the sacrificial system to Moses (Ceremonial laws). These were to form the basis of the religious ceremonies of the Israelites and to ensure that the Israelites' behavior reflected their status as God's chosen people.

Both sets of instructions were called the law, but they were different in that the law of Ten Commandments _____ what sin was, whereas the Ceremonial law contained the _____ to the sin problem.

The Mosaic law was given specifically to the nation of Israel (Ex. 19; Lev. 26:46; Rom. 9:4) in order to help them to worship God _____ and to treat one another with _____.

Traditionally, we refer to the first five books of the Old testament as law (Torah) but only four books contain these laws: Exodus, Leviticus, Numbers and Deuteronomy. The law in the Bible most often refers to the material found in **Exodus 20 – Deuteronomy 33**. The first five books also include narratives like the story of Moses in the basket.

The most well-known law literature in the Bible are the Ten Commandments found in Exodus 20:1-17 and Deuteronomy 5:6-20. In the New Testament, the Sermon on the Mount (Matt. 5-7) is considered law and the fulfillment of the law.

The Old Testament contains over _____ commandments which the Israelites were expected to keep as evidence of their _____ to God.

An important question

Are you expected as a Christian to keep the Old Testament law?

_____

_____

To better understand the nature of God and define which laws are still required to follow, the Jewish law has been divided by many theologians in _____ categories: Ceremonial Civil and Moral. The Bible itself does not divide the law into these categories (many of the laws overlap in their purpose), but this three-fold division is nevertheless useful when we talk about the laws.

1. The _____ **laws** (also known as Ritual laws) constitute the _____ portion of the Old Testament laws and include instructions for worship, sacrifice, dietary, and cleanliness.

Animal sacrifice is an important theme found throughout Scripture because "without the shedding of blood there is no forgiveness" (Hebrews 9:22 _NIV_). The animal served as a substitute—that is, the animal died in place of the sinner, but only temporarily, which is why the sacrifices needed to be offered over and over. The animal sacrifices provided a temporary covering of sins and were "only a **shadow** of the good things that are coming..." (Hebrews 4: 1 _NIV_).
The future things to come was the sacrifice of Jesus dying for us on the cross. "But he has appeared once for all at the culmination of the ages to do away with sin by the sacrifice of himself" (Hebrews 9:26 _NIV_).

The Ceremonial laws ended at the cross with the blood of Jesus and therefore, it is _____ to us.

2. The _____ **laws** are the _____ largest portion of the Old Testament laws. These laws address how the Israelites were to interact with one another and with others, and specify penalties for various crimes (major and minor). The Civil laws applied exclusively to citizens of ancient Israel. These laws dictated Israel's daily living (Deut. 24:10-11); but modern society and culture has changed so radically that they are _____ to us anymore. The principles behind the commands are used to guide our conduct. The Moral laws are the foundation of the Civil laws.

3. The _____ **laws** are the final and smallest portion of the Old Testament laws. They reveal the _____ and _____ of God, and _____ to us today. Since God does not change, neither do moral principles. A good example is the Ten Commandments (Ex 20:1-17).

It is clear that some stipulations of the Old Testament (Covenant) have clearly not been renewed in the New Testament (Covenant), like the Ceremonial laws and Civil laws. It is only the Moral laws that have been renewed in the New Covenant, since they are cited in various ways in the New Testament (Matt. 5:21-48; John 7:23).

Civil Laws	Ceremonial Laws	Moral Laws

PURPOSE

Civil Laws	Ceremonial Laws	Moral Laws
Regulating the nation of Israel	To make atonement for sin. Point to Christ, the true Lamb	Universal guidelines telling us how to live

EXAMPLE

Civil Laws	Ceremonial Laws	Moral Laws
Building regulations (Deut 22:8)	The Passover (Lev 16)	The Ten Command-ments (Ex 20)

It is important to know that all of the Old Testament law is still the _____ of God for us even though it is not the _____ of God to us.

It would be a big mistake to conclude that the law is no longer a valuable part of the Bible. It fulfilled a great function in the history of salvation to "bring us to Christ" (Gal. 3:22-25), by showing how high God's standards of righteousness are and how impossible it is to meet those standards apart from divine aid.

The law functioned exactly this way for the ancient Israelites as well. **The law was never given to _____ people. Only God could save them.** He alone provided their means of rescue from slavery in Egypt, their conquest of the land of Canaan, andprosperity as inhabitants of that promised land. The law did none of that. The law simply represented the terms of the agreement of loyalty that Israel had with God.

The law in that sense stands as a paradigm (model). It is hardly a complete list of all the things one could or should do to please God. The law, rather, presents examples of what it means to be _____ to God.

Bottom line: The law reminds us that we are not capable of keeping the law as "All have sinned and come short of the glory of God" (Rom. 3:23 *NIV*). That is what the law says. It shows us our utter helplessness and hopelessness, and that we are made right with God by placing our faith in Jesus Christ (Rom. 3:19-22). Jesus is the only One who, by the grace of God, can save us and deliver us, reconcile us with God, and make us safe for all eternity.

In the Old Covenant (Testament) the Israelites could only approach God through the animal sacrifices and the High Priest. In the New Covenant (Testament) Jesus has come and shed the blood of the New Covenant.

"This is my blood of the covenant, which is poured out for many for the forgiveness of sins" (Matthew 26:28 *NIV*).

The Old Covenant was established following the _____ whereas the New Covenant was established at the _____. In the Old Covenant the High Priest was the mediator between the Israelites and God wheras Jesus is the mediator of the New Covenant. In the New Covenant we have direct access to God through Jesus.

The Old Testament law as a benefit to Israel

Many of the prohibitions and requirements in the Old Testament, like the food laws do not make sense to the modern Western mind. We need to remember that the whole world in Moses' time was idolatrous, with each nation believing in many deities. The forbidding of certain foods was to distinguished Israel from the other nations as God's chosen people.

The Old Testament laws were an _____ over laws from the Ancient Near East. One example is that class distinctions were built into the laws of other nations; however, the Old Testament prohibitions do not distinguish between genders or social status.[1]

Although the law was not designed to provide eternal life and true righteousness before God, it still was _____ **to the Israelites**. The food laws, laws about shedding of blood and laws giving blessing to those who keep them are examples of God's grace to his people.

1. The food laws (Lev 17 and Deut 14)

Example: Leviticus 11:7
"And the pig, though it has a divided hoof, does not chew the cud; it is unclean for you." (NIV)

The problem is God did not provide them with a reason why certain foods could or could not be eaten. The vast majority of foods prohibited are those which are most likely to carry _____ in the arid climate of the Sinai desert. Pigs were also uneconomical to raise as food in their context. Those foods were also favored for religious sacrifices by groups whose practices the Israelites were not to copy.

2. Laws about the shedding of blood

Example: Exodus 29:10-12

[10] "Bring the bull to the front of the tent of meeting, and Aaron and his sons shall lay their hands on its head. [11] Slaughter it in the Lord's presence at the entrance to the tent of meeting. [12] Take some of the bull's blood and put it on the horns of the altar with your finger, and pour out the rest of it at the base of the altar." (NIV)

God _____ the death of an animal in place of the death of a human sinner. A substitute's blood could be shed. Moreover, the laws that required a substitutionary sacrifice "... are a shadow of the things that were to come; the reality, however, is found in Christ (Col 2:17 *NIV*).

3. Laws giving blessing to those who keep them

Example: Deuteronomy 14:28-29

[28] "At the end of every three years, bring all the tithes of that year's produce and store it in your towns, [29] so that the Levites (who have no allotment or inheritance of their own) and the foreigners, the fatherless and the widows who live in your towns may come and eat and be satisfied, and so that the Lord your God may bless you in all the work of your hands." (NIV)

This law provides _____ for the needy (the Old Testament welfare system was well-established), and benefits for those who benefit the needy.

Match the corresponding letter with the respective law

Civil laws match
____ and ____

A

"He must first bring a young bull for a sin offering and a ram for a burnt offering."
(Lev. 16:3 *NIV*)

D

[13] "You shall not murder. [14] You shall not commit adultery. [15] You shall not steal. [16] You shall not give false testimony against your neighbor." (Ex. 20 *NIV*)

Ceremonial laws match
____ and ____

B

"When you build a new house, make a parapet around your roof so that you may not bring the guilt of bloodshed on your house if someone falls from the roof." (Deut. 22:8 *NIV*

E

"Be kind and compassionate to one another, forgiving each other, just as in Christ God forgave you."
(Eph. 4:32 *NIV*)

Moral laws match
____ and ____

C

[10] "This is my covenant with you and your descendants after you, the covenant you are to keep: Every male among you shall be circumcised. [11] You are to undergo circumcision, and it will be the sign of the covenant between me and you." (Gen. 17:10-11 *NIV*)

F

"If anyone grazes their livestock in a field or vineyard and lets them stray and they graze in someone else's field, the offender must make restitution from the best of their own field or vineyard."
(Ex. 22:5 *NIV*)

How to analyze the Law?

1. Determine whether the passage is Ceremonial, Civil, or Moral Law

Reason: Only the Moral Law applies to us.

3.2 Mark the main themes.

Reason: To see how the author had arranged his thoughts.

How do we mark the main themes?
*You first **zoom in** to the passage by marking everything that relates. After you have marked everything that relates you **zoom out**.*

3.3 Conclude and summarize the message to the original receiver.

(Most of the time the message is explicit and direct.)

_____

_____

Leviticus 23: 26-32 (Prose: Law) The Day of Atonement

[26] Then the Lord said to Moses, [27] "Be careful to celebrate the Day of Atonement on the tenth day of that same month—nine days after the Festival of Trumpets. You must observe it as an official day for holy assembly, a day to deny yourselves and present special gifts to the Lord. [28] Do no work during that entire day because it is the Day of Atonement, when offerings of purification are made for you, making you right with the Lord your God. [29] All who do not deny themselves that day will be cut off from God's people. [30] And I will destroy anyone among you who does any work on that day. [31] You must not do any work at all! This is a permanent law for you, and it must be observed from generation to generation wherever you live. [32] This will be a Sabbath day of complete rest for you, and on that day you must deny yourselves. This day of rest will begin at sundown on the ninth day of the month and extend until sundown on the tenth day."

Questions for Group Discussion

- Did the lesson help you to get a better understanding of the Law?
- What touched you the most in the lesson?
- Why is it important to distinguish between the different laws of the Old Testament?
- Why are the Ceremonial and Civil laws not applicable to us anymore?
- Although many of the Old Testament laws are not applicable to us anymore, why is it still important to view them as God's Word to us?
- Is there anything in the lesson that was not clear to you? If so, what was unclear?
- Share blessings and prayer requests and pray for one another.

LESSON 5
THE GPS-METHOD APPLIED TO LEVITICUS 19:9-14

Purpose
To apply the GPS-Method to Leviticus 19:9-14

The Bible GPS-Method takes us through the processes of UNDERSTANDING, APPLICATION AND COMMUNICATION

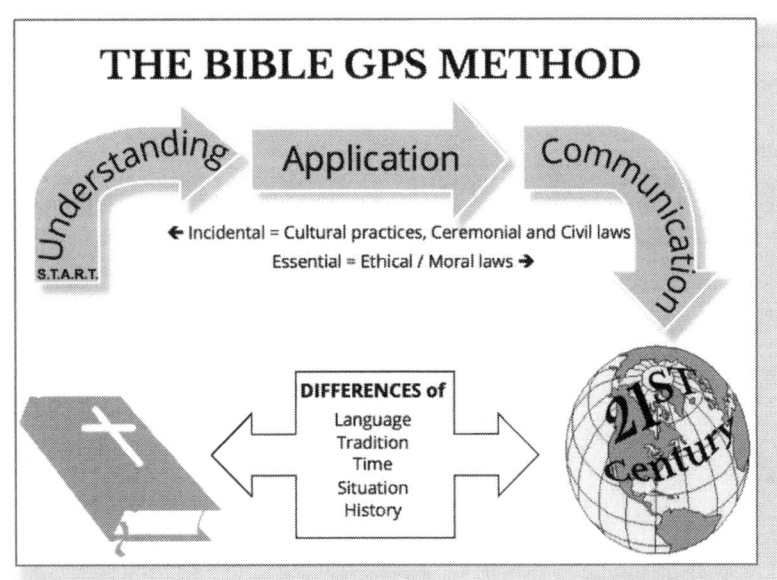

Leviticus 19:9-14

[9] "When you harvest the crops of your land, do not harvest the grain along the edges of your fields, and do not pick up what the harvesters drop. [10] It is the same with your grape crop—do not strip every last bunch of grapes from the vines, and do not pick up the grapes that fall to the ground. Leave them for the poor and the foreigners living among you. I am the Lord your God.

[11] Do not steal.
Do not deceive or cheat one another.

[12] Do not bring shame on the name of your God by using it to swear falsely. I am the Lord.

[13] Do not defraud or rob your neighbor.
"Do not make your hired workers wait until the next day to receive their pay.

[14] Do not insult the deaf or cause the blind to stumble. You must fear your God; I am the Lord." (NLT)

A. THE PROCESS OF UNDERSTANDING (S.T.A.R.T.)

1. SITUATION

The context of a passage will help you better understand the text. You can get the information from a Study Bible, Bible commentaries or from the Internet: http://www.biblestudytools.com/leviticus/

- **What was the purpose of the book?**

  _____

- **Who was the Sender and Receiver?**

  _____

- **Where does the passage fit in the structure (division) of the specific book?**

  A. The Five Main Offerings (1:1-7:38)
  B. The ordination of the priests (8:1-10:20)
  C. The Distinction Between Clean and Unclean (11:1-15:32)
  D. The Annual Day of Atonement (16:1-34)
  E. Prescriptions for Practical Holiness (17:1-26:46)
  F. Regulations for Offerings Vowed to the Lord (27:1-34)

• Where does the passage fit in the structure (division) of the Bible?

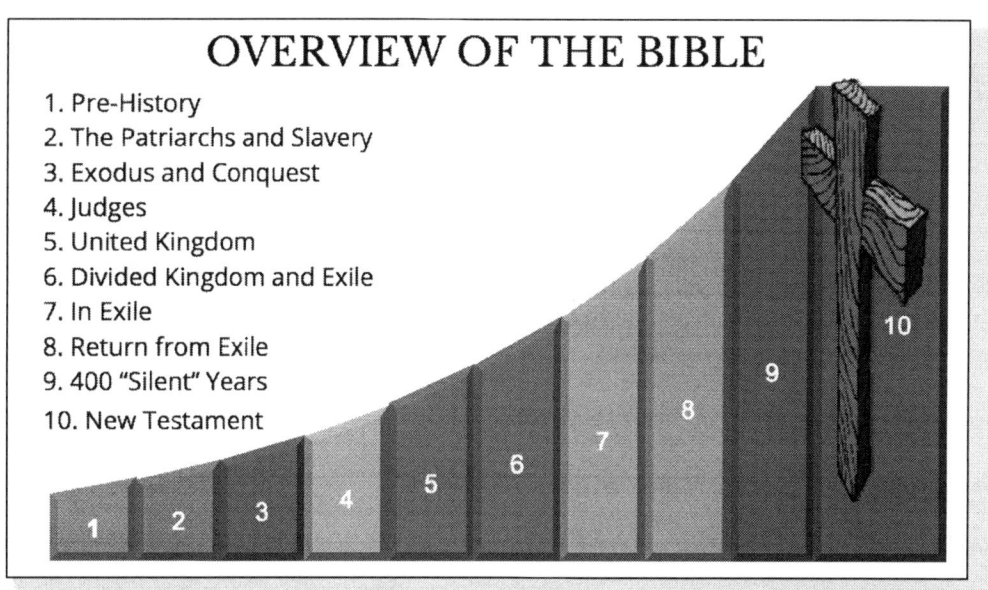

OVERVIEW OF THE BIBLE

1. Pre-History
2. The Patriarchs and Slavery
3. Exodus and Conquest
4. Judges
5. United Kingdom
6. Divided Kingdom and Exile
7. In Exile
8. Return from Exile
9. 400 "Silent" Years
10. New Testament

• When did the book originate?

_____

• Placing of the book?

_____

• Important characters

_____

• Distinctive features

_____

2. TYPE OF LITERATURE

The type of literature will determine how you will analyze the passage.

PROSE	POETRY
Narrative/History The Law Prophecy Gospel Epistle (Letter) Apocalyptic Writing	Wisdom Psalms Prophecy

What type of literature is Leviticus 19:9-14?

_____

3. ANALYSIS OF THE PASSAGE

3.1 Determine whether the passage is Ceremonial, Civil, or Moral Law.

Reason: Only the Moral Law applies to us.

3.2 Mark the main themes.
Reason: To see how the author had arranged his thoughts.

How do we mark the main themes?
*You first **zoom in** to the passage by marking everything that relates. After you have marked everything that relates you **zoom out**.*

3.3 Conclude and summarize the message to the original receiver.
(Most of the time the message is explicit and direct.)

God asks them to act in good manner in all spheres of life. It is, therefore, clear that everything in their lives involves God.

4. RELATIONSHIP TO THE REST OF THE BIBLE

Does the message in Leviticus 19:9-14 relate to the rest of the Bible?

Read the following passages to determine your answer:

Matthew 23:23 (NLT)

23 "What sorrow awaits you teachers of religious law and you Pharisees. Hypocrites! For you are careful to tithe even the tiniest income from your herb gardens, but you ignore the more important aspects of the law— justice, mercy, and faith. You should tithe, yes, but do not neglect the more important things."

1 Peter 1:14-16 (NLT)

"14 So you must live as God's obedient children. Don't slip back into your old ways of living to satisfy your own desires. You didn't know any better then. 15 But now you must be holy in everything you do, just as God who chose you is holy. 16 For the Scriptures say, "You must be holy because I am holy."

Romans 3:23 (NIV)

"for all have sinned and fall short of the glory of God,"

YES _____ NO _____

5. TEST OF YOUR FINDINGS

Do the findings of other sources (e.g., commentaries, Study Bibles) confirm the message to the original receiver?

YES _____ NO _____

B. THE PROCESS OF APPLICATION

In this process, we determine whether or not the message to the original receiver is still applicable (essential or incidental) to our present situation.

You must distinguish the difference between an INCIDENTAL and an ESSENTIAL message.

We saw in Module 1, Lesson 4 (pages 67-71) that only the Moral (Ethical) Laws are essential and, therefore, applicable to us.

Civil Laws	Ceremonial Laws	Cultural Practices	Moral Laws

PURPOSE

Civil Laws	Ceremonial Laws	Cultural Practices	Moral Laws
Regulating the nation of Israel	Animal sacrifices to make atonement for sin. Point to Christ, the true Lamb	Comprise the ways people do certain things	Universal guidelines telling us how to live

EXAMPLE

Civil Laws	Ceremonial Laws	Cultural Practices	Moral Laws
Building regulations (Deut 22:8)	The Passover (Lev 16)	To greet with a kiss. (1 Peter 5:14)	The Ten Commandments (Ex 20)

Is the message to the original receivers applicable to us in the 21st century?

YES _____ NO _____

C. THE PROCESSES OF COMMUNICATION

In this process we communicate the message to a specific target group.

Read this devotional.

Should Everything in Life Involve God?

During service on Sunday, the sermon and hymns make us aware of God's presence and that worship involves God. However, during the course of the week, we tend to focus on other things and forget about God. The question is: Should everything in life involve God? The following section will help answer this question.

Nearly all of the warnings in Leviticus 19 are written in the form of commands (Do not . . .).

In this section, God admonishes His people to be holy. This theme is of such importance in the book that the word "holy" is used 152 times. God wanted the Israelites to lead a holy life, because this would serve as a testimony to other nations that He was holy. But what does it mean to be holy? Thomas Carlyle said: "The old word for holy in the German language, heilig, also means healthy. And so heilbronn means holy-well, or healthy-well. You could not get any better definition of what holy really is than healthy—completely healthy."

But how were they to live in order to reflect God's holiness? Leviticus 17–26, known as the Law of Holiness, is the most important part of the book. These chapters contain instructions about how to dedicate oneself to God. For instance, Leviticus 18 refers to sexual relationships, while in Leviticus 19, God orders the Israelites to do things that will make them holy, such as show respect to their parents (v. 3), not curse the deaf (v. 14) and treat the elderly with respect (v. 32).
God asks us to act in a holy manner in all spheres of life. It is therefore clear that everything in our lives involves God.

(Taken from the Devotional "From a Garden to a City.")

Questions for Group Discussion

1. The result of a holy lifestyle is a healthy society. How do you rate the health of your society on a scale of 1 to 10, where 10 is best? Why do you rate your society in this way?

_____

_____

2. Do you think Christians take "holiness" seriously enough? Please explain your answer.

_____

_____

3. Read the following passages. What do these passages say about holiness?

- 1 Thessalonians 4:3-7

_____

- Ephesians 4:22-24

_____

4. Share blessings and prayer requests and pray for one another.

"Holiness is not the luxury of a few people, but a simple duty for you and me."
Mother Teresa

LESSON 6
THE GPS-METHOD APPLIED TO Deuteronomy 15:12-17

Purpose
To apply the GPS-Method to DEUTERONOMY 15:12-17

The Bible GPS-Method takes us through the processes of UNDERSTANDING, APPLICATION AND COMMUNICATION

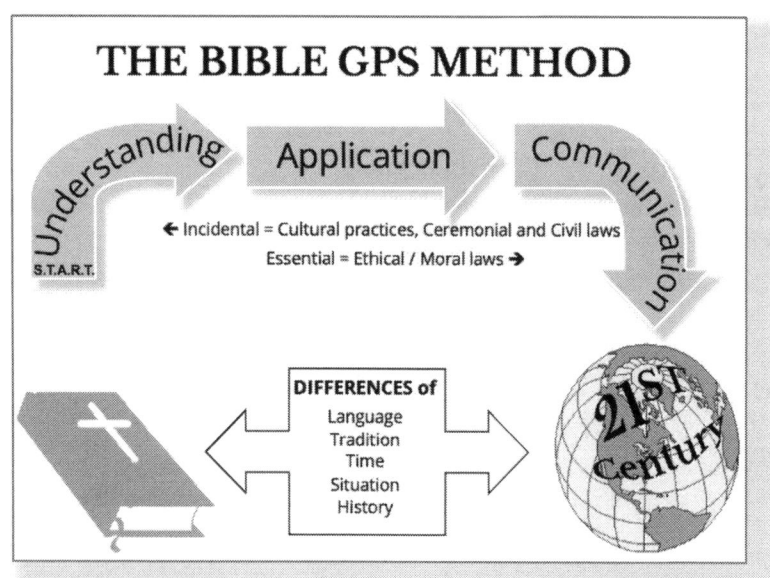

Deuteronomy 15:12-17

[12] "If a fellow Hebrew sells himself or herself to be your servant and serves you for six years, in the seventh year you must set that servant free.

[13] When you release a male servant, do not send him away empty-handed. [14] Give him a generous farewell gift from your flock, your threshing floor, and your winepress. Share with him some of the bounty with which the Lord your God has blessed you. [15] Remember that you were once slaves in the land of Egypt and the Lord your God redeemed you! That is why I am giving you this command.

[16] But suppose your servant says, 'I will not leave you,' because he loves you and your family, and he has done well with you. [17] In that case, take an awl and push it through his earlobe into the door. After that, he will be your servant for life. And do the same for your female servants." (NLT)

A. THE PROCESS OF UNDERSTANDING (S.T.A.R.T.)

1. SITUATION

The context of a passage will help you better understand the text. You can get the information from a Study Bible, Bible commentaries or from the Internet: http://www.biblestudytools.com/deuteronomy/

- **What was the purpose of the book?**

  _____

- **Who was the Sender and Receiver?**

  _____

- **Where does the passage fit in the structure (division) of the specific book?**

  A. Preamble (1:1-5)
  B. Historical Prologue (1:6; 4:43)
  C. Stipulations of the Covenant (4:44; 26:19)
  D. Ratification; Curses and Blessings (chs. 27-30)
  E. Leadership Succession under the Covenant (chs. 31-34)

- Where does the passage fit in the structure (division) of the Bible?

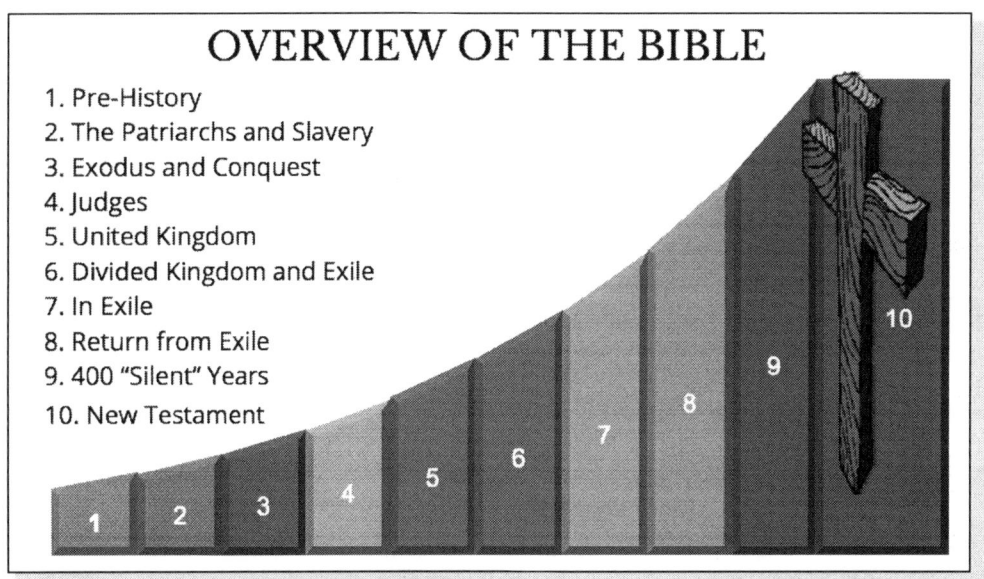

OVERVIEW OF THE BIBLE

1. Pre-History
2. The Patriarchs and Slavery
3. Exodus and Conquest
4. Judges
5. United Kingdom
6. Divided Kingdom and Exile
7. In Exile
8. Return from Exile
9. 400 "Silent" Years
10. New Testament

- When did the book originate?

_____

- Placing of the book?

_____

- Important characters

_____

- Distinctive features

_____

2. *T*ype of literature

The type of literature will determine how you will analyze the passage.

PROSE	POETRY
Narrative/History The Law Prophecy Gospel Epistle (Letter) Apocalyptic Writing	Wisdom Psalms Prophecy

What type of literature is Deuteronomy 15:12-17?

_____

3. ANALYSIS OF THE PASSAGE

3.1 Determine whether the passage is Ceremonial, Civil, or Moral Law.

Reason: Only the Moral Law applies to us.

3.2 Mark the main themes.
Reason: To see how the author had arranged his thoughts.

How do we mark the main themes?
*You first **zoom in** to the passage by marking everything that relates. After you have marked everything that relates you **zoom out**.*

3.3 Conclude and summarize the message to the original receiver.
(Most of the time the message is explicit and direct.)

The instructions required in this passage clearly indicate that God values every person. These instructions needed to remind the Israelites that they were also slaves earlier in Egypt and that their freedom is a gift from God.

4. RELATIONSHIP TO THE REST OF THE BIBLE

Does the message in Deuteronomy 15:12-17 relate to the rest of the Bible?

Read the following passages to determine your answer:

Matthew 7:12 (NIV)
"So in everything, do to others what you would have them do to you, for this sums up the Law and the Prophets."

Romans 12:10 (NIV)
"Be devoted to one another in love. Honor one another above yourselves."

YES _____ NO _____

5. TEST OF YOUR FINDINGS

Do the findings of other sources (e.g., commentaries, Study Bibles) confirm the message to the original receiver?

YES _____ NO _____

B. THE PROCESS OF APPLICATION

In this process, we determine whether or not the message to the original receiver is still applicable (essential or incidental) to our present situation.

You must distinguish the difference between an INCIDENTAL and an ESSENTIAL message.

We saw in Module 1, Lesson 4 (pages 67-71) that only the Moral (Ethical) Laws are essential and, therefore, applicable to us.

Civil Laws	Ceremonial Laws	Cultural Practices	Moral Laws

PURPOSE

Regulating the nation of Israel	Animal sacrifices to make atonement for sin. Point to Christ, the true Lamb	Comprise the ways people do certain things	Universal guidelines telling us how to live

EXAMPLE

Building regulations (Deut 22:8)	The Passover (Lev 16)	To greet with a kiss. (1 Peter 5:14)	The Ten Commandments (Ex 20)

Is the message to the original receivers applicable to us in the 21st century?

YES _____ NO _____

C. THE PROCESSES OF COMMUNICATION

In this process we communicate the message to a specific target group.

Questions for Group Discussion

1. Although the law of Deuteronomy is not a command directly to us or about us, we can learn many things from this law. Israel's legal code was unique. The other nations' ancient law codes favored the elite, the wealthy, and the royal. Israel's law favored the weak, socially and economically deprived, legally vulnerable, and disenfranchised!

What does this legal code reveal about God?

_____

_____

2. What do you think is the state of the weak, socially and economically deprived, legally vulnerable, and disenfranchised people in your country? What do you think can and should be done in order to address these challenges?

_____

_____

3. Letting slaves go free after six years of service provided a major limitation on the practice of slavery, and ensured the practice could not be abused beyond reasonable limits (Deut. 15:12). God's provision for slavery was not a brutal regulation and, therefore, we cannot use this passage to justify the harsh practices of slavery of the past. Slavery, as practiced at that time, was quite different from what we usually think of as slavery.

We hereby see that God loves slaves and His love is seen in the safeguards built into the law.

Why was it important for Israel to remember that they were once slaves in the land of Egypt?

_____

_____

4. We learn in verses 16-17 that the slaves could actually be better off in bondage than free. The slave had access to food, clothing, and shelter, on their own they might die of starvation. God wanted people to be treated with respect and dignity (see also Philemon 1).

What is the situation in your society? What role can we play to make our societies better and healthier?

_____

_____

5. One of the most famous chimpanzees of all time is Washoe, who was picked up by soldiers in West Africa. In 1966, two doctors who raised her almost like a child, adopted her. In 1970, however, she was turned over to another pair of doctors and taken to the University of Oklahoma. Here she went through rigorous training to become the first non-human to learn American Sign Language. She learned over 140 signs! It was discovered, however, that she was just mimicking all that she had been taught. After several years, the staff decided that she was able to try to conceptualize. "She is going to say what is on her heart!" the staff declared. In her safe and secure cage, well taken care of, Washoe said the first three words of her own initiative: "**LET ME OUT**!!!" She signed these words several times. **Even in animals, there is a desire for freedom**. Given the opportunity, most animals would leave safety for the chance of freedom. Humans long for freedom as well. We yearn to enjoy life, free from guilt and despair. We want to live significant lives. Moreover, God has created us for freedom—it is our intended destiny.

In Deuteronomy 15:15 we read: "Remember that you were once slaves in the land of Egypt and the Lord your God redeemed you!"

How does God eventually redeem us in the New Testament in the light of the following two passages?

"So Christ has truly set us free. Now make sure that you stay free, and don't get tied up again in slavery to the law." (Gal 5:1 NLT)

"So now there is no condemnation for those who belong to Christ Jesus. 2 And because you belong to him, the power of the life-giving Spirit has freed you from the power of sin that leads to death." (Rom. 1:1-2 NLT)

_____

_____

6. Share blessings and prayer requests and pray for one another

About the Author

KOBUS GENIS was born in Bellville, South Africa. He obtained a Bachelor's Degree in Theology (BTh) from the University of Stellenbosch, South Africa, and served as a minister in South Africa from 1992-2003.
Since 2003 he and his family have been living in sunny Alberta, Canada, where he is a minister at Westminster Presbyterian Church, Calgary. Kobus' passion is to teach people how to UNDERSTAND, APPLY and COMMUNICATE the essentials of the Bible in the 21st century.

He is the author of two Devotionals: *From a Garden to a City* and *@Godstweet* as well as a discipleship book: *The Bible GPS.*

www.thebiblegps.com
https://www.facebook.com/BibleGPS

BIBLE
GPS

Devotionals by the Author

Two Devotional Books Complement the Meet GOD Modules

From a Garden to a City

(365 devotionals) will take you on an exciting journey through all the Bible Books. This journey follows the story line of the Bible that begins in Genesis in the GARDEN of Eden and ends in Revelation with a CITY, the New Jerusalem.

Visit https://thebiblegps.com for more information.

@GodsTweet is a daily devotional

that will take you on an exciting journey through all the Bible books. @GodsTweet consists of 170 devotionals that will help you to get a better understanding of the Bible.

Visit https://thebiblegps.com for more information.

COUPON

GPS2

Made in the USA
Middletown, DE
10 September 2019